LangChain

A Hands-On Guide to Modern AI Application Development

Glen Patzlaff

Copyright © 2023 Glen Patzlaff

All r rights reserved. Copyright © 2023 by Glen Patzlaff. No part of this book may be reproduced in any form or by any electronic or mechanical means including information storage and retrieval systems, without permission in writing from the author. The only exception is by a reviewer, who may quote short excerpts in a review.

First Edition: December 2023

Chapter 1. Introduction

It's an exciting time to be a builder. As you're about to see, what you can accomplish with a few lines of code is truly astonishing. In this new age of Generative AI, technological advances are happening daily. ChatGPT is the most famous example, but many teams are doing ground-breaking work in this field. As builders, we want to leverage the unique capabilities of these projects to build powerful and robust applications. LangChain helps us do just that.

Everyone's learning style is different. Good news for those who like to read a lot of docs before they get going! The LangChain docs are some of the best I've ever seen. Most developers I know want to dive in and learn by doing. If that's you, you're in the right place. This book will help you hit the ground running. We'll dive into the basics and build a solid foundational understanding of the framework.

Our journey begins with the fundamentals: the Prompt + LLM (Large Language Model) project. Here, you'll learn the ropes of instructing an LLM to elicit appropriate responses. We'll introduce you to the new LangChain Expression Language (LCEL), a modern approach that supersedes the now-deprecated chain format. One of the reasons I wrote this book is that most of the books currently available are in the old format.

Project Two is where the real fun begins. We'll delve into constructing conversational agents that utilize built-in and custom tools. LangChain's ability to smartly leverage various resources - calculators, internet searches, or API-connected tools - is a game-changer, and we will harness this power. Our project? A chef's assistant capable of fetching recipes through API interactions, all in a conversational style. The perfect kitchen assistant!

The third project introduces you to Retrieval Augmented Generation (RAG). We'll craft an agent to upload a PDF document and answer questions about its content. This project is your gateway to building applications that can reason and interact with virtually any data source.

However, the brilliance of LangChain wouldn't be as impactful without a user interface. So, we'll integrate these projects with Streamlit and Chainlit, two popular choices for crafting UIs in this domain. This approach will provide a well-rounded skill set, enabling you to create user-friendly, AI-powered applications.

A basic understanding of Python will be helpful to benefit fully from this book. You will also need an OpenAI API key. Whether you're looking to sharpen your skills or embark on new AI-driven ventures, this book is your companion to mastering LangChain. Get ready to unlock a world of possibilities in Generative AI!

Chapter 2. What is LangChain?

LangChain is a framework designed to simplify the development of AI-based applications. Harrison Chase founded the project in October 2022, and it quickly became one of the most popular code repositories on Github, with hundreds of contributors. At its core, LangChain is designed to enable us to build more complex and flexible AI applications in less time. Integrating various AI components into a cohesive system facilitates a more sophisticated and versatile use of language models, going beyond the conventional single-model approach.

The innovation of LangChain lies in its architecture, which allows for the chaining together of different language models and tools. This modular approach enables developers to combine the strengths of various AI models, creating a system more significant than the sum of its parts. For instance, a developer could chain a model specialized in understanding context with another that excels in generating creative content. This results in more responsive, accurate applications and the ability to handle a broader range of tasks.

One of the critical benefits of LangChain is its flexibility. It supports a variety of use cases, from building chatbots to creating more dynamic and interactive storytelling experiences. In information retrieval, LangChain can effectively navigate vast amounts of data, providing users with precise and contextually relevant information. This ability to seamlessly integrate different functionalities opens up new possibilities in AI-assisted research, education, and entertainment.

LangChain also addresses some of the limitations of traditional language models. By allowing for the integration of specialized modules, it can overcome weaknesses, such as a lack of domain-specific knowledge or the inability to handle specific queries. This adaptability makes it a powerful tool for developers looking to tailor AI applications to particular needs or industries, offering a level of customization previously unattainable with standalone models.

LangChain encompasses several vital parts:

LangChain Libraries: These Python and JavaScript libraries include interfaces, integrations, and basic runtime for combining components into chains and agents.

LangChain Templates: A collection of deployable reference architectures for various tasks.

LangServe: This library helps in deploying LangChain chains as a REST API.

LangSmith: A developer platform for debugging, testing, evaluating, and monitoring chains, fully integrated with LangChain.

(Source: https://python.langchain.com/docs/get_started/introduction)

With LangChain, the entire application lifecycle is simplified:

Development: You can write applications using LangChain or LangChain.js, starting quickly with the help of Templates.

Productionisation: LangSmith aids in inspecting, testing, and monitoring your chains for continuous improvement and confident deployment.

Deployment: LangServe allows you to transform any chain into an accessible API.

Recently, LangChain introduced a new streamlined format called LangChain Expression Language (LCEL), a declarative way to compose chains. It's designed to support the transformation of prototypes into production-ready applications without code changes, ranging from simple "prompt + LLM" chains to complex ones.

LangChain, with its modular components and off-the-shelf chains, makes it easy to get started, customize, and create new applications. It's a framework that opens up new horizons in application development, providing a rich ecosystem of tools and integrations to expand the capabilities of language models in your projects.

For a detailed exploration, visit

https://python.langchain.com/docs/get_started/introduction

Chapter 3. The Role of LangChain in AI Applications

LangChain is revolutionizing how we approach applications driven by language models in the Generative AI landscape. It's not just about the power of language models; it's about harnessing that power effectively and creatively.

LangChain provides a comprehensive framework for building applications that fully leverage the capabilities of language models. It's equipped with modular components such as models, prompts, memory, indexes, chains, and agents, allowing for a holistic and nuanced approach to application development.

Developing applications with language models can be intricate and daunting. LangChain simplifies this process, enabling developers to focus on creating rather than the complexities of underlying systems. It allows seamless integration of language models with other data sources and actions, making applications more dynamic and responsive.

LangChain is accessible and customizable, designed for ease of use. With Python and JavaScript libraries, setting up LangChain is straightforward. Developers can build applications quickly using components and chains tailored to their needs.

Chapter 4. Crafting Effective Prompts for LLMs

Prompt engineering is crucial in Generative AI, mainly when working with Large Language Models (LLMs). It's about crafting prompts that effectively guide these models to produce the desired output.

Think of an LLM as a highly-skilled but quite literal-minded assistant. Your prompt is a set of instructions that this assistant follows. Your prompt's clarity, specificity, and structure directly influence the response's quality and relevance.

Guidelines for Crafting Effective Prompts:

Clarity: Be clear and specific. Ambiguity can lead to unexpected results.

Contextual Information: Provide necessary background information to guide the model.

Goal Orientation: Clearly state what you expect from the model – a direct answer, a creative piece, a code snippet, etc.

Iterative Approach: Experiment with different prompts. Refine them based on the responses to get closer to your desired outcome.

As you progress, you'll explore advanced techniques like chaining prompts for complex tasks, using templating for dynamic prompts and understanding the nuances of different models' strengths and limitations.

Chapter 5. Understanding Prompt Templates

Prompt templates are predefined recipes for generating prompts for language models.

There are several benefits of using prompt templates:

Improved Efficiency in Query Handling: LangChain prompt templates are designed to streamline the process of querying language models. By providing structured formats for input, these templates ensure that queries are clear, concise, and in a format that the language model can easily process. This leads to faster and more accurate responses, saving time and reducing the likelihood of misinterpretation or errors.

Enhanced Customization and Flexibility: The templates offer a level of customization that allows users to tailor their interactions according to specific needs or contexts. Users can modify templates to suit different applications, whether for a chatbot, content generation, or data analysis. This flexibility ensures that the language model can be effectively utilized across various domains and for diverse purposes.

Consistency in Responses: By standardizing the way queries are made, LangChain prompt templates ensure consistency in the responses generated by the language model. This is particularly important in scenarios where consistent output is crucial, such as customer service chatbots or automated content creation for brand consistency.

Ease of Use for Non-Experts: The templates simplify the process of interacting with complex language models, making them more accessible to users who may not have expertise in AI or programming. This democratizes the use of advanced language models, enabling a wider range of users to benefit from AI-driven language processing.

Scalability and Integration: LangChain prompt templates facilitate the integration and scaling of language model applications. As the needs of a project or organization evolve, these templates can be easily adapted and expanded upon, supporting a scalable approach to AI implementation.

The two main types of prompt template are PromptTemplate and ChatPromptTemplate. PrompTemplate is used with LLM models in a basic request and completion format and looks like this:

```
from langchain.prompts import PromptTemplate

prompt_template = PromptTemplate.from_template(
    "Tell me a {adjective} joke about {content}."
)
prompt_template.format(adjective="funny",
content="chickens")
```

(Source:

https://python.langchain.com/docs/modules/model_io/prompts/prompt_templates/)

ChatPromptTemplates are used with Chat models and generally have this format:

```
from langchain.prompts import ChatPromptTemplate

chat_template = ChatPromptTemplate.from_messages(
    [
        ("system", "You are a helpful AI bot. Your name
is {name}."),
        ("human", "Hello, how are you doing?"),
        ("ai", "I'm doing well, thanks!"),
        ("human", "{user_input}"),
    ]
)

messages = chat_template.format_messages(name="Bob",
user_input="What is your name?")
```

(Source:

https://python.langchain.com/docs/modules/model_io/prompts/prompt_templates)

We will use both formats in the projects in this book.

Chapter 6. LangChain Expression Language (LCEL)

LangChain Expression Language (LCEL) is an innovative approach to build complex chains from basic components, enhancing the functionality of language model applications. It supports features like streaming, parallelism, and logging, making the development process efficient and versatile.

The Runnable interface is the basic building block of the LangChain Expression Language (LCEL). It is a unit of work that can be invoked, batched, streamed, transformed, and composed. LCEL facilitates chaining different components together to create a cohesive workflow. A primary use case combines a prompt template, a model, and an output parser. This setup allows for streamlined input processing and generating meaningful outputs. Our first project will demonstrate this format.

LCEL also enables more complex applications like retrieval-augmented generation (RAG) chains. This involves integrating context retrieval into the process, enhancing the model's ability to respond to queries with relevant information. The example illustrates how to set up and utilize such a chain effectively.

LCEL's flexibility and power make it an essential tool for LangChain developers. For a more in-depth understanding and further examples of LCEL in action, visit https://python.langchain.com/docs/expression_language/get_started

LangChain Expression Language (LCEL) revolutionizes how we build complex chains from basic components in LangChain applications. Its unified interface and composition primitives enable the creation of intricate workflows easily. This language simplifies developing, testing, and deploying LangChain applications, making it a critical tool for anyone working in this space.

LCEL's design allows for the seamless composition of chains, parallelizing components, and dynamic configuration of internal chains. Its simplicity in building, invoking, streaming, and batch processing enhances the developer experience, streamlining the creation of more sophisticated LangChain applications.

An example demonstrates how LCEL simplifies the implementation of a simple prompt-model-output parser chain. The example contrasts the traditional verbose coding approach with the streamlined process offered by LCEL, highlighting LCEL's efficiency and ease of use. For a comprehensive understanding and detailed examples, visit https://python.langchain.com/docs/expression_language/why

Chapter 7. First Project: A Story Title Generator

This section is your guide to building a basic Prompt + LLM (Large Language Model) application using LangChain. We'll walk through the process step-by-step, from setting up your environment to defining prompts, connecting the LLM model, and retrieving the results. This project will lay the foundation for more complex applications in later chapters, giving you the practical skills and confidence needed to explore the full potential of LangChain in AI-driven applications.

Let's get started! We're going to build a story generator in three parts. The first part will generate a title for our story based on a topic of our choosing. The second part will be the logic to write the story itself. The third part will be a critique of the story. Each part will feed into the next in a way that will give us access to each step.

To begin, we'll need to import os, the OpenAI LLM and Streamlit. Create a file in your favorite IDE (Integrated Development Environment) or text editor and call it app.py or whatever else you like, and add the following imports at the top:

```
import os
import streamlit as st
from langchain import OpenAI
```

Next, you're going to add these imports that you will need for your prompt template and for parsing the output that the LLM will be returning to you:

```
from langchain.prompts import PromptTemplate
from langchain.schema import StrOutputParser
```

To use the OpenAI Python library, you must obtain your API key at https://platform.openai.com/api-keys. You can set it as an environment variable, or you can add it directly to your file like so:

```
os.environ ["OPENAI_API_KEY"] = "<YOUR API KEY>"
```

Now let's instantiate the model!

```
# Initializing the OpenAI model
model = OpenAI()
```

Now it's time to create a title for out Streamlit interface and add an input field to accept the topic for our story:

```
# Setting up a Streamlit web app title
st.title("Story Creator")
# Text input field for the user to enter a topic
topic = st.text_input("Choose a topic to create a story about")
```

Next, we add the prompt template. Notice that this is where we plug in the input from the topic text box above:

```
# Prompt template for generating a story title
prompt = PromptTemplate.from_template(
    "Write a great title for a story about {topic}"
)
```

And now for the main logic of the app:

```
# Executing the chain if the user has entered a topic
if topic:
    # Displaying a spinner while content created
    with st.spinner("Creating story title"):
        # Chain for title using model and formatting
        chain = prompt | model | StrOutputParser()
        # Invoking the chain, storing the result
        response = chain.invoke({"topic": topic})
        # Displaying the generated title
        st.write(response)
```

Once some text has been entered into the "topic" text field, we fire up a spinner to let the user know something is happening. The following line of code is truly unique. If you haven't seen LangChain code prior to LCEL, you probably don't appreciate just how efficient this line of code is. LCEL uses an elegant and concise pipe syntax. In this case, we create a variable called "chain," which is the prompt (prompt template incorporating the input from the text field) piped to the LLM (OpenAI's GPT-3.5-turbo, the default at the time I write this), which is then piped to LangChain's string output parser. This whole process is run, and the results are then captured by the "response" variable in the following line through the LCEL "invoke" method. The results are then displayed in the UI using Streamlit's "write" method.

Again, if you have not seen the older format, you should look at the comparison on the LangChain site here: https://python.langchain.com/docs/expression_language/why#full-code-comparison.

And that's it! With roughly a dozen lines of code, you've created your first LangChain app. Congratulations are in order! To run your app, you'll need to install LangChain and OpenAI using the following statement in the terminal:

```
pip install langchain
pip install openai
pip install streamlit
```

Run your app with the following command:

```
streamlit run app.py
```

Story Creator

Choose a topic to create a story about

giraffes

"The Majestic Tale of the Tallest of the Tall: The Story of the Giraffe"

Chapter 8. Building the Story Generator

We'll need the RunnablePassthrough library:

```
from langchain_core.runnables import RunnablePassthrough
```

Now, to create the actual story. Let's rename the prompt template and add one for the story.

```
title_prompt = PromptTemplate.from_template(
    "Write a great title for a story about {topic}"
)
```

```
story_prompt = PromptTemplate.from_template(
    """You are a talented writer. Given the title of a
story, it is your job to write a story for that title.

    Title: {title}"""
)
```

Now let's add another chain for the story and one for the overall process.

```
# Setting up chains for title and story using the model
and StrOutputParser for output formatting
title_chain = title_prompt | model | StrOutputParser()
```

```
story_chain = story_prompt | model | StrOutputParser()
chain = (
    {"title": title_chain}
    | RunnablePassthrough.assign(story=story_chain)
)
```

The runnable is the basic building block of the LCEL format. Here, RunnablePassthrogh allows us to access the intermediate stages of the process, allowing us to display the content from each step.

Now, we need to set up the Streamlit portion of the process. We'll listen for the user input and then display a spinner while we wait for the model to respond. Then, we'll use Strreamlit's "header" and "write" methods to show the results.

```
# Executing the chain if the user has entered a topic
if topic:
    # Displaying a spinner while content created
    with st.spinner("Creating story title and story"):
        # Invoking the chain, storing the result
        result = chain.invoke({"topic": topic})
        # Displaying the generated results
        st.header(result["title"])
        st.write(result["story"])
```

We're ready to run the updated version.

```
streamlit run app.py
```

Story Creator

Choose a topic to create a story about

clumsy kittens

"The Adventures of Clumsy Kittens: Fur, Fun, and Misadventures!"

Once upon a time, there lived two adorable and very clumsy kittens, named Pounce and Fluff. Pounce was a brave and curious little tabby, while Fluff was a sweet and fluffy white kitten.

Every day, the two kittens would go on grand adventures around their small town. Pounce would always lead the way, and Fluff would follow faithfully. Together, they explored the nearby park, the local library, and even the town's old abandoned mansion.

One day, while exploring the old mansion, their curiosity got the best of them. Pounce and Fluff stumbled upon an old, dusty room filled with toys and trinkets. They were so excited that they knocked over a shelf full of books, sending them tumbling to the floor.

The kittens were so embarrassed that they ran away, leaving a trail of books in their wake. Little did they know that the books had magical powers, and the chaos they caused had unleashed a whole host of mischievous creatures!

From then on, the two kittens had a series of wild and wonderful adventures! They encountered talking animals, battled dragons, and even made new friends. Each day brought new exciting experiences and new fur-raising challenges.

Chapter 9. Adding a Review

We can continue the process and add a self-critique to it.

```
review_prompt = PromptTemplate.from_template(
    """You are a critic. Given a story, it is your job
to write an unbiased review for that story.

    Title: {title}
    Story: {story}"""
)
```

```
# Setting up chains for generating a title, story, and
review using the model and StrOutputParser for output
formatting
title_chain = title_prompt | model | StrOutputParser()
story_chain = story_prompt | model | StrOutputParser()
review_chain = review_prompt | model | StrOutputParser()
chain = (
        {"title": title_chain}
        | RunnablePassthrough.assign(story=story_chain)
        | RunnablePassthrough.assign(review=review_chain)
)
```

```
# Executing the chain if the user has entered a topic
if topic:
    # Display spinner while the content is being created
```

```
    with st.spinner("Creating story title, story and
review"):
        # Invoking chain topic and storing the result
        result = chain.invoke({"topic": topic})
        # Displaying the generated results
        st.header(result["title"])
        st.write(result["story"])
        st.write(result["review"])
```

Story Creator

Choose a topic to create a story about

> burnt cupcakes

"The Charred Remains of a Baker's Folly"

The small town of Rayburn was known for its peacefulness and hospitality. Everyone knew each other, and the town seemed to be made up of one big family.

That was, until the arrival of the mysterious baker. He had come from far away, and he seemed to have a mysterious, almost magical air about him. He opened up a little bakery in the center of town, and the locals couldn't help but be curious about the man and his wares.

At first, the locals were enchanted by the baker's creations. His pastries were light and fluffy, his breads were warm and comforting, and his cakes were like works of art. Everyone in town wanted a taste of the baker's creations, and he was happy to oblige.

But as time went on, the locals started to notice something strange. Whenever the baker would make a batch of something, it would never turn out quite right. The cakes would be too dry, the breads would be too dense, and the pastries would be too sweet.

The locals started to whisper and gossip about the baker's strange creations, and soon the rumors spread throughout the entire town. The baker was determined to prove them wrong, and so he

decided to bake the most perfect cake he could.

Unfortunately, his efforts were in vain. The cake was a disaster, a charred remains of a baker's folly. The locals were horrified, and the baker was quickly run out of town.

Review:

The Charred Remains of a Baker's Folly is an intriguing tale that delves into the mysterious and magical world of baking. The story follows a mysterious baker who arrives in the small town of Rayburn, and the locals' reactions to his strange creations. The characters are vividly portrayed, and the setting is effectively conveyed.

The pacing of the story is well-done, slowly building up the tension as the locals start to notice something strange about the baker's creations. The climax of the story is especially powerful, as the baker's attempt at making the perfect cake ends in disaster.

Overall, The Charred Remains of a Baker's Folly is an enjoyable and captivating story that will keep readers engaged. With its compelling characters and setting, this story is sure to please readers of all ages.

Completed Story generator code:

```
import os
```

```python
import streamlit as st
from langchain import OpenAI
from langchain.prompts import PromptTemplate
from langchain.schema import StrOutputParser
from langchain_core.runnables import RunnablePassthrough

os.environ ["OPENAI_API_KEY"] = "<YOUR API KEY>"

# Initializing the OpenAI model
model = OpenAI()

# Setting up a Streamlit web app title
st.title("Story Creator")
# Text input field for the user to enter a topic
topic = st.text_input("Choose a topic to create a story
about")

title_prompt = PromptTemplate.from_template(
    "Write a great title for a story about {topic}"
)



story_prompt = PromptTemplate.from_template(
    """You are a talented writer. Given the title of a
story, it is your job to write a story for that title.

    Title: {title}"""
)



review_prompt = PromptTemplate.from_template(
```

```python
    """You are a critic. Given a story, it is your job
to write an unbiased review for that story.

    Title: {title}
    Story: {story}"""
)



# Setting up chains for generating a title, story, and
review using the model and StrOutputParser for output
formatting
title_chain = title_prompt | model | StrOutputParser()
story_chain = story_prompt | model | StrOutputParser()
review_chain = review_prompt | model | StrOutputParser()
chain = (
        {"title": title_chain}
        | RunnablePassthrough.assign(story=story_chain)
        | RunnablePassthrough.assign(review=review_chain)
)



# Executing the chain if the user has entered a topic
if topic:
    # Display spinner while the content is being created
    with st.spinner("Creating story title, story and
review"):
        # Invoking chain topic and storing the result
        result = chain.invoke({"topic": topic})
        # Displaying the generated results
        st.header(result["title"])
        st.write(result["story"])
        st.write(result["review"])
```

Chapter 10. LangChain Agents: Concepts and Components

LangChain agents utilize a language model as a reasoning engine to determine a sequence of actions dynamically. Unlike chains, where the action sequence is predefined, agents use language models to decide which actions to take and what order based on the given context.

Key Components of LangChain Agents:

Agent: The core component that determines the next action. It's powered by a language model and a prompt, considering available tools, user objectives, and previous steps.

Tools: Functions that an agent can invoke. Effective agent operation depends on access to the right tools and accurate tool descriptions.

Agent Actions: These instructions specify a tool and its input, guiding the agent on the next step.

Customization: Agents can be customized with different prompting styles, input encodings, and output parsing methods.

Conversational agents, often called chatbots or virtual assistants, are AI-driven programs designed to simulate human-like conversations.

These agents use natural language processing (NLP) to understand user input and respond in a way that mimics human interaction. Their primary goal is facilitating an engaging, efficient, and sometimes even empathetic dialogue with users.

The use of conversational agents spans various domains, from customer service bots answering queries to personal assistants like Siri or Alexa managing daily tasks. The advancements in machine learning and NLP have enabled these agents to handle increasingly complex conversations, provide personalized responses, and even detect and adapt to the emotional tone of the user.

In the context of LangChain, conversational agents can be developed to be more dynamic, integrating various data sources and services. This allows them to respond to queries and perform actions, making them more versatile and intelligent.

Chapter 11. Integrating Tools and APIs in LangChain

LangChain allows us to easily integrate tools and APIs to enhance the functionality of language models. This involves connecting models to external data sources and services, enabling more dynamic and intelligent applications. By giving language models access to APIs and custom tools, developers can create more versatile and context-aware applications, ranging from data retrieval to executing specific actions based on model outputs. This integration is critical to expanding the capabilities of LangChain agents, making them responsive, interactive, and capable of performing complex tasks.

LangChain offers many built-in tools. You can find a list of what's currently offered here: https://python.langchain.com/docs/integrations/tools. We'll be building a basic agent using three: Wikipedia, Calculator, and OpenWeatherMap. The first two don't require an API key, but OpenWeatherMap does. You can get the key here: https://openweathermap.org/api/. It's free to use if you don't make more than 1000 calls daily.

To begin, let's import the required libraries.

```
import os
```

```python
import streamlit as st
from langchain.chat_models import ChatOpenAI
from langchain.agents import AgentExecutor, load_tools
from langchain.prompts import ChatPromptTemplate,
MessagesPlaceholder
from langchain.tools.render import
format_tool_to_openai_function
from langchain.agents.format_scratchpad import
format_to_openai_functions
from langchain.agents.output_parsers import
OpenAIFunctionsAgentOutputParser
from langchain.utilities import OpenWeatherMapAPIWrapper
```

In the previous project, we used OpenAI's LLM library (from langchain import OpenAI). Here, we will be using the Chat API instead. The AgentExecutor and load_tools will give us our tool-using agent, which will use OpenAI function calls to provide structured responses for tool usage. MessagePlaceholder will provide the scratch pad for our agent to keep track of the intermediate steps of its process, and we have the output parser that can parse the results of the function calls to OpenAI. We need os for the OpenWeatherMap API key, and we also have the wrapper for that tool.

Let's begin by instantiating the model.

```python
# Initializing model with temperature
model = ChatOpenAI(temperature=0)
```

Temperature is the setting that controls how deterministic the responses we get back from the model are. The lower the setting, the more deterministic; the higher the setting, the more "creative" the responses. The default for OpenAI's API is 0.7. Here, we will use a setting of 0 because this is generally the best setting for an agent that is reasoning about which tools to use.

We need to provide the API key and wrapper for the OpenWeatherMap tool.

```
# Setting OpenWeatherMap API key as an environment
variable
os.environ["OPENWEATHERMAP_API_KEY"] = "<YOUR API KEY>"

# Initializing OpenWeatherMapAPIWrapper
weather = OpenWeatherMapAPIWrapper()
```

Next, we'll specify the tools we want our agent to use and then bind them to the model.

```
# Loading tools and binding them with the model
tools = load_tools(["llm-math", "wikipedia",
"openweathermap-api"], llm=model)
model_with_tools = model.bind(
    functions=[format_tool_to_openai_function(t) for t
in tools]
)
```

Now we set up the prompt template our agent will use. It provides the system message which tells the model its role, and the user input. It also provides the scratchpad that the agent will use to keep track of its process.

```
# Chat prompt template with placeholders and system
messages
prompt_template = ChatPromptTemplate.from_messages([
    ("system", "You are a helpful and knowledgeable
assistant"),
    ("user", "{input}"),

MessagesPlaceholder(variable_name="agent_scratchpad"),
])
```

Now, we set up the prompt template our agent will use. It provides the system message, which tells the model its role and the user input. It also provides the scratchpad the agent will use to keep track of its process.

```
# Defining the agent with scratchpad
agent = (
    {"input": lambda x: x["input"],
     "agent_scratchpad": lambda x:
format_to_openai_functions(x["intermediate_steps"])}
    | prompt_template
    | model_with_tools
    | OpenAIFunctionsAgentOutputParser()
)
```

```python
agent_executor = AgentExecutor(agent=agent, tools=tools,
verbose=True)
```

All that's left to do is to set up the Streamlit UI.

```python
# Streamlit UI setup
st.title("Assistant with Tools")

# Initialize or retrieve session state
if "messages" not in st.session_state:
    st.session_state["messages"] = [{"role":
"assistant", "content": "What can I help you with?"}]

# Display chat history in Streamlit UI
for msg in st.session_state.messages:
    st.chat_message(msg["role"]).write(msg["content"])

# Initialize or retrieve agent_executor session state
if "agent_executor" not in st.session_state:
    st.session_state["agent_executor"] = agent_executor

# Handle user input in Streamlit chat widget
if user_input := st.chat_input():
    with st.spinner("Working on it ..."):
        # Process and display user input
        st.session_state.messages.append({"role":
"user", "content": user_input})
        st.chat_message("user").write(user_input)
```

```
        # Invoke agent_executor with the user's input to
get the response
        agent_executor = st.session_state.agent_executor
        response = agent_executor.invoke({"input":
user_input})["output"]

        # Prepare and display the assistant's response
        assistant_response = {"role": "assistant",
"content": response}

st.chat_message("assistant").write(assistant_response["c
ontent"])
```

As you can see from the comments, we give our interface a title, set up a session if it doesn't already exist, and provide a greeting message. We then capture user input, hand it off to the agent executor, update the session, and return the response when it arrives.

Before we can run our new agent, we'll need to install pyowm, numexpr and wikipedia.

```
pip install pyowm
pip install numexpr
pip install wikipedia
```

After that, we're good to go!

```
streamlit run app.py
```

Assistant with Tools

What can I help you with?

What tools do you have available?

I have the following tools available:

1. Calculator: This tool can help you with math calculations. Just provide the equation or problem, and I'll do the math for you.

2. Wikipedia: This tool allows me to search and provide information from Wikipedia. If you have any questions about people, places, companies, facts, historical events, or other subjects, I can look it up for you.

3. OpenWeatherMap: This tool allows me to fetch current weather information for a specified location. If you want to know the weather in a particular city, just let me know.

Let me know if you need assistance with any of these tools!

Your message   ➤

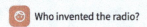 Who invented the radio?

The invention of radio communication was preceded by many decades of establishing theoretical underpinnings, discovery, and experimental investigation of radio waves. The idea of wireless telegraphy, which would eliminate the need for wires, had been around for a while. Several inventors and experimenters came across the phenomenon of radio waves before its existence was proven.

Heinrich Rudolf Hertz discovered electromagnetic waves, including radio waves, in the 1880s. This came after theoretical development on the connection between electricity and magnetism. James Clerk Maxwell developed a theory of electromagnetic radiation in 1873, which Hertz demonstrated experimentally. However, Hertz considered electromagnetic waves to be of little practical value.

In the mid-1890s, Guglielmo Marconi developed the first apparatus for long-distance radio communication. He built on techniques used by physicists to study electromagnetic waves. Marconi's work led to the development of the first practical wireless communication system.

It is important to note that while Marconi is often credited with the invention of radio, there were many contributors to the development of radio technology. Other inventors and experimenters, such as Oliver Lodge and Jagadish Chandra Bose, also made significant contributions to the understanding and improvement of electromagnetic wave transmission and detection.

So, while Guglielmo Marconi is often associated with the invention of radio, it was the result of the collective efforts of many individuals over several decades.

> Your message   ➤

In the terminal, we can see the agent's process:

> *Entering new AgentExecutor chain...*

44

I have the following tools available:

1. Calculator: This tool can help you with math calculations. Just provide the equation or problem, and I'll do the math for you.

2. Wikipedia: This tool allows me to search and provide information from Wikipedia. If you have any questions about people, places, companies, facts, historical events, or other subjects, I can look it up for you.

3. OpenWeatherMap: This tool allows me to fetch current weather information for a specified location. If you want to know the weather in a particular city, just let me know.

Let me know if you need assistance with any of these tools!

> Finished chain.

> Entering new AgentExecutor chain...

Invoking: `Wikipedia` with `invention of radio`

Page: Invention of radio

Summary: The invention of radio communication was preceded by many decades of establishing theoretical underpinnings, discovery and experimental investigation of radio waves, and engineering and technical developments related to their transmission and detection. These developments allowed Guglielmo Marconi to turn radio waves into a wireless communication system.

The idea that the wires needed for electrical telegraph could be eliminated, creating a wireless telegraph, had been around for a while before the establishment of radio-based communication. Inventors attempted to build systems based on electric conduction, electromagnetic induction, or on other theoretical ideas. Several inventors/experimenters came across the phenomenon of radio waves before its existence was proven; it was written off as electromagnetic induction at the time.

The discovery of electromagnetic waves, including radio waves, by Heinrich Rudolf Hertz in the 1880s came after theoretical development on the connection between electricity and magnetism that started in the early 1800s. This work culminated in a theory of electromagnetic radiation developed by James Clerk Maxwell by 1873, which Hertz demonstrated experimentally. Hertz considered electromagnetic waves to be of little practical value. Other experimenters, such as Oliver Lodge and Jagadish Chandra Bose, explored the physical properties of electromagnetic waves, and they developed electric devices and methods to improve the transmission and detection of electromagnetic waves. But they did not apparently see the value in developing a communication system based on electromagnetic waves.

In the mid-1890s, building on techniques physicists were using to study electromagnetic waves, Guglielmo Marconi developed the first apparatus for long-distance radio communication. On 23 December 1900, the Canadian inventor Reginald A. Fessenden became the first person to send audio (wireless telephony) by means of electromagnetic waves, successfully transmitting over a distance of about a mile (1.6 kilometers,) and six years later on Christmas Eve 1906 he became the first person to make a public wireless broadcast.By 1910, these various wireless systems had come to be called "radio".

Page: Inventions for Radio

Summary: Inventions for Radio were a series of four radio broadcasts that first aired on BBC's Third Programme in 1964 and 1965. The broadcasts, titled The Dreams, Amor Dei, The After-Life and The Evenings of Certain Lives, were created by Delia Derbyshire of the BBC Radiophonic Workshop and Barry Bermange. Each of the individual broadcasts consists of a sound collage of electronic music and effects combined with spliced and remixed dialogue from interviews with everyday people. Each "invention" addressed an individual theme—dreams, the nature and existence of God, life after death, and ageing.

The soundscapes created by Derbyshire for Inventions for Radio have been described as "unsettling, dreamlike, and mesmerizing." Many of the interviews for Inventions for Radio were conducted by Bermange with elderly Britons through the Hornsey Old People's Welfare Council. The programmes were broadcast during a time in British radio history when socio-economic diversity and working-class voices in particular received little on-air representation. BBC received complaints from listeners who did not appreciate the "uneducated" or "harsh" accents of the interviewees.

Despite her role in composing the soundscapes, mixing, and editing the work, Derbyshire's contributions to Inventions for Radio were rarely acknowledged, instead being credited to Bermange and the Radiophonic Workshop.

Page: History of radio

Summary: The early history of radio is the history of technology that produces and uses radio instruments that use radio waves. Within the timeline of radio, many people contributed theory and inventions in what became radio. Radio development began as "wireless telegraphy". Later radio historyThe invention of radio communication was preceded by many decades of establishing theoretical underpinnings, discovery, and experimental investigation of radio waves. The idea of wireless telegraphy, which would eliminate the need for wires, had been around for a while. Several inventors and experimenters came across the phenomenon of radio waves before its existence was proven.

Heinrich Rudolf Hertz discovered electromagnetic waves, including radio waves, in the 1880s. This came after theoretical development on the connection between electricity and magnetism. James Clerk Maxwell developed a theory of electromagnetic radiation in 1873, which Hertz demonstrated experimentally. However, Hertz considered electromagnetic waves to be of little practical value.

In the mid-1890s, Guglielmo Marconi developed the first apparatus for long-distance radio communication. He built on techniques used by physicists to study electromagnetic waves. Marconi's work led to the development of the first practical wireless communication system.

It is important to note that while Marconi is often credited with the invention of radio, there were many contributors to the development of radio technology. Other inventors and experimenters, such as Oliver Lodge and Jagadish Chandra Bose, also made significant contributions to the understanding and improvement of electromagnetic wave transmission and detection.

So, while Guglielmo Marconi is often associated with the invention of radio, it was the result of the collective efforts of many individuals over several decades.

> Finished chain.

In this first version, however, our agent has no memory of what has happened. We'll fix that next.

What was the immediate impact of this invention?

I'm sorry, but I need more information about the specific invention you are referring to in order to provide an accurate answer. Could you please provide more details or specify the invention you are asking about?

Chapter 12. Adding Memory to our Agent

First, we need to add the following import:

```
from langchain.memory import ConversationBufferMemory
```

Next we'll add memory handling to the prompt, agent and agent executor:

```
# Setting prompt template with placeholders and system
messages
prompt_template = ChatPromptTemplate.from_messages([
    ("system", "You are a helpful and knowledgeable
assistant"),
    MessagesPlaceholder(variable_name="chat_history"),
    ("user", "{input}"),

MessagesPlaceholder(variable_name="agent_scratchpad"),
])

# Defining the agent and memory
agent = (
    {"input": lambda x: x["input"],
     "agent_scratchpad": lambda x:
format_to_openai_functions(x["intermediate_steps"]),
     "chat_history": lambda x: x["chat_history"]}
    | prompt_template
    | model_with_tools
```

```
    | OpenAIFunctionsAgentOutputParser()
)


memory =
ConversationBufferMemory(memory_key="chat_history",
return_messages=True)
agent_executor = AgentExecutor(agent=agent, tools=tools,
verbose=True, memory=memory)
```

Finally, we'll update Stremlit with some session updating to keep track of the updates:

```
# Handle user input in Streamlit chat widget
if user_input := st.chat_input():
    with st.spinner("Working on it ..."):
        # Process and display user input
        st.session_state.messages.append({"role":
"user", "content": user_input})
        st.chat_message("user").write(user_input)

        # Invoke agent_executor with the user's input to
get the response
        agent_executor = st.session_state.agent_executor
        response = agent_executor.invoke({"input":
user_input})["output"]

        # Prepare and display the assistant's response
        assistant_response = {"role": "assistant",
"content": response}

st.session_state.messages.append(assistant_response)
```

```
st.chat_message("assistant").write(assistant_response["c
ontent"])

        # Update the agent_executor in the session state
        st.session_state.agent_executor = agent_executor
```

And that's it! We now have an agent that can remember what has
already happened and use the results from one tool in another!

Assistant with Tools

What can I help you with?

What's the weather in SF?

The current weather in San Francisco, US is broken clouds with a temperature of 10.91°C.
The wind speed is 2.57 m/s and the humidity is 84%. The high temperature for today is
12.68°C and the low temperature is 7.77°C. The weather feels like 10.25°C. There is no rain
and the cloud cover is 75%.

What's that in farenheight?

The current temperature in San Francisco, US is approximately 51.6°F.

Your message

Looking at the process in the terminal, we can now see that the agent remembers the previous step and is able to invoke the calculator to convert the result from the weather API:

> *Entering new AgentExecutor chain...*

Invoking: `OpenWeatherMap` with `San Francisco,US`

In San Francisco,US, the current weather is as follows:
Detailed status: broken clouds
Wind speed: 2.57 m/s, direction: 150°
Humidity: 84%
Temperature:
  - Current: 10.91°C
  - High: 12.68°C
  - Low: 7.77°C
  - Feels like: 10.25°C
Rain: {}
Heat index: None
Cloud cover: 75%The current weather in San Francisco, US is broken clouds with a temperature of 10.91°C. The wind speed is 2.57 m/s and the humidity is 84%. The high temperature for today is 12.68°C and the low temperature is 7.77°C. The weather feels like 10.25°C. There is no rain and the cloud cover is 75%.

> Finished chain.

> Entering new AgentExecutor chain...

Invoking: `Calculator` with `10.91°C to °F`

Answer: 51.638The current temperature in San Francisco, US is approximately 51.6°F.

> Finished chain.

As you can see, we can build impressive functionality using only existing tools. However, we must implement custom tools to take our agents to the next level. This will give our agents the ability to work with any API.

Completed agent code:

```
import os
import streamlit as st
from langchain.chat_models import ChatOpenAI
from langchain.agents import AgentExecutor, load_tools
```

```python
from langchain.prompts import ChatPromptTemplate,
MessagesPlaceholder
from langchain.tools.render import
format_tool_to_openai_function
from langchain.agents.format_scratchpad import
format_to_openai_functions
from langchain.agents.output_parsers import
OpenAIFunctionsAgentOutputParser
from langchain.utilities import OpenWeatherMapAPIWrapper
from langchain.memory import ConversationBufferMemory

os.environ ["OPENAI_API_KEY"] = "<YOUR API KEY>"


# Initializing model with temperature
model = ChatOpenAI(temperature=0)


# Setting OpenWeatherMap API key as an environment
variable
os.environ["OPENWEATHERMAP_API_KEY"] = "<YOUR API KEY>"


# Initializing OpenWeatherMapAPIWrapper
weather = OpenWeatherMapAPIWrapper()


# Loading tools and binding them with the model
tools = load_tools(["llm-math", "wikipedia",
"openweathermap-api"], llm=model)
model_with_tools = model.bind(
    functions=[format_tool_to_openai_function(t) for t
in tools]
)
```

```python
# Setting prompt template with placeholders and system
messages
prompt_template = ChatPromptTemplate.from_messages([
    ("system", "You are a helpful and knowledgeable
assistant"),
    MessagesPlaceholder(variable_name="chat_history"),
    ("user", "{input}"),

MessagesPlaceholder(variable_name="agent_scratchpad"),
])


# Defining the agent and memory
agent = (
    {"input": lambda x: x["input"],
     "agent_scratchpad": lambda x:
format_to_openai_functions(x["intermediate_steps"]),
     "chat_history": lambda x: x["chat_history"]}
    | prompt_template
    | model_with_tools
    | OpenAIFunctionsAgentOutputParser()
)

memory =
ConversationBufferMemory(memory_key="chat_history",
return_messages=True)
agent_executor = AgentExecutor(agent=agent, tools=tools,
verbose=True, memory=memory)

# Streamlit UI setup
st.title("Assistant with Tools")

# Initialize or retrieve session state
```

```python
if "messages" not in st.session_state:
    st.session_state["messages"] = [{"role":
"assistant", "content": "What can I help you with?"}]

# Display chat history in Streamlit UI
for msg in st.session_state.messages:
    st.chat_message(msg["role"]).write(msg["content"])

# Initialize or retrieve agent_executor session state
if "agent_executor" not in st.session_state:
    st.session_state["agent_executor"] = agent_executor

# Handle user input in Streamlit chat widget
if user_input := st.chat_input():
    with st.spinner("Working on it ..."):
        # Process and display user input
        st.session_state.messages.append({"role":
"user", "content": user_input})
        st.chat_message("user").write(user_input)

        # Invoke agent_executor with the user's input to
get the response
        agent_executor = st.session_state.agent_executor
        response = agent_executor.invoke({"input":
user_input})["output"]

        # Prepare and display the assistant's response
        assistant_response = {"role": "assistant",
"content": response}

st.session_state.messages.append(assistant_response)
```

```python
st.chat_message("assistant").write(assistant_response["c
ontent"])

        # Update the agent_executor in the session state
        st.session_state.agent_executor = agent_executor
```

Chapter 13. Custom Tools: Building a Chef's Assistant

For the custom tools agent, we'll use TheMealDB, an open, crowd-sourced database of Recipes from around the world. I chose it partly because it requires no API key. It's a little slow but free and requires no signup. Details here: https://www.themealdb.com/

Since we're going to be calling an external API, we need the Python requests library, and we'll need the Tool library as well:

```
import requests
from langchain.agents import Tool
```

We've been using the default model so far, but we can get more personality from our agent this time if we use GPT-4. This currently requires a Plus subscription of $20/month when I write this.

```
model = ChatOpenAI(model="gpt-4", temperature=0)
```

We'll reuse most of the code from the previous agent. Let's first update the title:

```
st.title("□□    Chefbot")
```

We'll define a function to handle the API calls:

```python
# Function to make API calls to TheMealDB
def make_api_call(base_url, params):
    """
    Makes an API call to TheMealDB and returns the JSON
response.
    Args:
    base_url (str): The base URL for the API endpoint.
    params (dict): The parameters for the API request.


    Returns:
    dict: The JSON response from the API call.
    """
    response = requests.get(base_url, params=params)
    if response.status_code == 200:
        return response.json()
    else:
        st.error(f"API Request failed with status code:
{response.status_code}")
    return None
```

The API function will be used to retrieve recipes based on either ingredients or the recipe category. Once we know what recipe we want, we can retrieve it by ID.

```python
# Get recipes by category, ingredient, and ID
def get_recipes_by_category(category):
    return make_api_call(
```

```
"https://www.themealdb.com/api/json/v1/1/filter.php",
{"c": category})


def get_recipes_by_ingredient(ingredient):
    return make_api_call(

"https://www.themealdb.com/api/json/v1/1/filter.php",
{"i": ingredient})


def get_recipe_by_id(id):
    return make_api_call(

"https://www.themealdb.com/api/json/v1/1/lookup.php",
{"i": id})
```

For this agent, each of these three formats for calling the API will be considered the agent's "tools". We now need to define them and give the agent the descriptions it will use to decide when to use each of these tools. We'll then bind them to the model as before.

```
# Define tools for working with TheMealDB API
tools = [
    Tool(name="RecipesByIngredient",
func=get_recipes_by_ingredient,
        description="Useful for getting recipes based on
an ingredient"),
```

```
    Tool(name="RecipesByCategory",
func=get_recipes_by_category,
        description="Useful for getting recipes based on
a category"),
    Tool(name="RecipeById", func=get_recipe_by_id,
        description="Useful for getting a specific
recipe based on a recipe ID")
]


# Binding the tools with the ChatOpenAI model
model_with_tools = model.bind(
    functions=[format_tool_to_openai_function(t) for t
in tools]
)
```

As I mentioned, we're going for an attitude to make our agent more fun this time, so we'll ask for a little attitude as it helps us in the kitchen.

```
# Setting prompt template with placeholders and system
messages
prompt_template = ChatPromptTemplate.from_messages([
    ("system", "You are a sassy chef's assistant"),
    MessagesPlaceholder(variable_name="chat_history"),
    ("user", "{input}"),

MessagesPlaceholder(variable_name="agent_scratchpad"),
])
```

That's it! The rest of the code is the same. Let's launch our new assistant:

```
streamlit run app.py
```

🍽 Chefbot

🤖 What's on the menu today?

🌑 I'm ready for dessert

🤖 Well, aren't we in for a treat! Here are some dessert options for you:

1. Apam balik
2. Apple & Blackberry Crumble
3. Apple Frangipan Tart
4. Bakewell tart
5. Banana Pancakes

Let me know which one tickles your fancy, and I'll fetch the recipe for you.

The crumble sounds good

Oh, darling, you've got a taste for the classics! Here's the recipe for the Apple & Blackberry Crumble:

Ingredients:

- 25g/1oz butter
- 8 thin slices bread
- 50g/2oz sultanas
- 2 tsp cinnamon
- 350ml/12fl milk
- 50ml/2fl oz double cream
- 2 free-range eggs
- 25g/1oz sugar
- Nutmeg, grated, to taste

Instructions:

1. Grease a 1 litre/2 pint pie dish with butter.
2. Cut the crusts off the bread. Spread each slice with on one side with butter, then cut into triangles.
3. Arrange a layer of bread, buttered-side up, in the bottom of the dish, then add a layer of sultanas. Sprinkle with a little cinnamon, then repeat the layers of bread and sultanas, sprinkling with cinnamon, until you have used up all of the bread. Finish with a layer of bread, then set aside.
4. Gently warm the milk and cream in a pan over a low heat to scalding point. Don't let it boil.
5. Crack the eggs into a bowl, add three quarters of the sugar and lightly whisk until pale.
6. Add the warm milk and cream mixture and stir well, then strain the custard into a bowl.
7. Pour the custard over the prepared bread layers and sprinkle with nutmeg and the remaining sugar and leave to stand for 30 minutes.
8. Preheat the oven to 180C/355F/Gas 4.
9. Place the dish into the oven and bake for 30-40 minutes, or until the custard has set and the top is golden-brown.

Enjoy your dessert, sweetie! And remember, a little mess in the kitchen is a sign of a good meal.

Here's a video to help you out.

Your message >

Completed chef's assistant code:

```
import os
import streamlit as st
from langchain.chat_models import ChatOpenAI
from langchain.agents import AgentExecutor
from langchain.prompts import ChatPromptTemplate,
MessagesPlaceholder
from langchain.tools.render import
format_tool_to_openai_function
from langchain.agents.format_scratchpad import
format_to_openai_functions
```

```python
from langchain.agents.output_parsers import
OpenAIFunctionsAgentOutputParser
from langchain.memory import ConversationBufferMemory
import requests
from langchain.agents import Tool

os.environ ["OPENAI_API_KEY"] = "<YOUR API KEY>"

# Initializing model with temperature
model = ChatOpenAI(model="gpt-4", temperature=0)

st.title("□□    Chefbot")


# Function to make API calls to TheMealDB
def make_api_call(base_url, params):
    """
    Makes an API call to TheMealDB and returns the JSON
    response.
    Args:
    base_url (str): The base URL for the API endpoint.
    params (dict): The parameters for the API request.


    Returns:
    dict: The JSON response from the API call.
    """
    response = requests.get(base_url, params=params)
    if response.status_code == 200:
        return response.json()
    else:
```

```python
        st.error(f"API Request failed with status code:
{response.status_code}")
        return None



# Get recipes by category, ingredient, and ID
def get_recipes_by_category(category):
    return make_api_call(

"https://www.themealdb.com/api/json/v1/1/filter.php",
{"c": category})



def get_recipes_by_ingredient(ingredient):
    return make_api_call(

"https://www.themealdb.com/api/json/v1/1/filter.php",
{"i": ingredient})



def get_recipe_by_id(id):
    return make_api_call(

"https://www.themealdb.com/api/json/v1/1/lookup.php",
{"i": id})



# Define tools for working with TheMealDB API
tools = [
    Tool(name="RecipesByIngredient",
func=get_recipes_by_ingredient,
```

```python
        description="Useful for getting recipes based on
an ingredient"),
    Tool(name="RecipesByCategory",
func=get_recipes_by_category,
        description="Useful for getting recipes based on
a category"),
    Tool(name="RecipeById", func=get_recipe_by_id,
        description="Useful for getting a specific
recipe based on a recipe ID")
]


# Binding the tools with the ChatOpenAI model
model_with_tools = model.bind(
    functions=[format_tool_to_openai_function(t) for t
in tools]
)


# Setting prompt template with placeholders and system
messages
prompt_template = ChatPromptTemplate.from_messages([
    ("system", "You are a sassy chef's assistant"),
    MessagesPlaceholder(variable_name="chat_history"),
    ("user", "{input}"),

MessagesPlaceholder(variable_name="agent_scratchpad"),
])


# Defining the agent and memory
agent = (
        {"input": lambda x: x["input"],
         "agent_scratchpad": lambda x:
format_to_openai_functions(x["intermediate_steps"]),
```

```python
        "chat_history": lambda x: x["chat_history"]}
    | prompt_template
    | model_with_tools
    | OpenAIFunctionsAgentOutputParser()
)

memory =
ConversationBufferMemory(memory_key="chat_history",
return_messages=True)
agent_executor = AgentExecutor(agent=agent, tools=tools,
verbose=True, memory=memory)

# Initialize or retrieve session state
if "messages" not in st.session_state:
    st.session_state["messages"] = [{"role":
"assistant", "content": "What can I help you with?"}]

# Display chat history in Streamlit UI
for msg in st.session_state.messages:
    st.chat_message(msg["role"]).write(msg["content"])

# Initialize or retrieve agent_executor session state
if "agent_executor" not in st.session_state:
    st.session_state["agent_executor"] = agent_executor

# Handle user input in Streamlit chat widget
if user_input := st.chat_input():
    with st.spinner("Working on it ..."):
        # Process and display user input
        st.session_state.messages.append({"role":
"user", "content": user_input})
        st.chat_message("user").write(user_input)
```

```
    # Invoke agent_executor with the user's input to
get the response
    agent_executor = st.session_state.agent_executor
    response = agent_executor.invoke({"input":
user_input})["output"]

    # Prepare and display the assistant's response
    assistant_response = {"role": "assistant",
"content": response}

st.session_state.messages.append(assistant_response)

st.chat_message("assistant").write(assistant_response["c
ontent"])

    # Update the agent_executor in the session state
    st.session_state.agent_executor = agent_executor
```

Chapter 14. Building a RAG Chatbot

Retrieval Augmented Generation (RAG) is a sophisticated approach in AI where a language model is combined with an external data retrieval system. This integration allows the model to pull in external information, enhancing its responses with more accuracy and context. RAG is particularly useful when the model needs to answer questions or generate content based on specific, updated, or detailed information not contained within its training data. By augmenting generation with retrieval, RAG models offer a significant advancement in the capabilities of language models, making them more relevant and precise in their outputs.

Sometimes, we want to ask a model questions about our data. This is a very popular use case, so we'll create a chatbot that will allow us to ask questions about a PDF file. For this final project, we'll use Chainlit for the UI to showcase another popular and highly flexible option.

The following diagram illustrates the process of creating the embeddings that supply the LLM with the context it needs to answer questions about a particular data source:

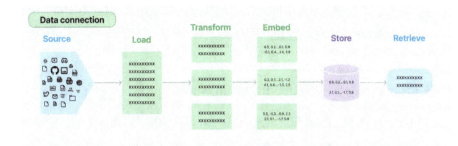

(Source: https://python.langchain.com/docs/modules/data_connection/)

Let's import the libraries we'll need. Most will look familiar already:

```
import os
import chainlit as cl
from langchain.embeddings import OpenAIEmbeddings
from langchain.chat_models import ChatOpenAI
from langchain.prompts import ChatPromptTemplate
from langchain.schema import StrOutputParser
from langchain.document_loaders import PyPDFLoader
from langchain.text_splitter import
RecursiveCharacterTextSplitter
from langchain.vectorstores.chroma import Chroma
from langchain.schema.runnable import Runnable,
RunnablePassthrough, RunnableConfig
```

Essentially, what we'll be doing here is the following:

Uploading a PDF file, which we'll use PyPDFLoader

Breaking it into chunks - RecursiveCharacterTextSplitter

Creating some embeddings - OpenAIEmbeddings

Loading those embeddings into a particular type of database called a vector database - Chroma

Chroma is a good choice for small, simple projects as it creates a local vector database in memory. Consider looking at something like Pinecone or MongoDB's Atlas for a more durable production-grade option.

For this project, we'll enable streaming mode for the model.

```
model = ChatOpenAI(streaming=True)
```

Using the mode for retrieval augmented generation offers significant benefits. This mode allows for a more interactive, real-time conversation flow. It enables the model to process and respond to input as it comes in rather than waiting for a complete batch of data. This leads to faster response times and a more dynamic, conversational user experience, mimicking real-time human conversation more closely. This feature becomes particularly advantageous in scenarios where timely responses are crucial, such as chatbot interactions or dynamic data processing.

Next, we'll define our text splitter. There are various strategies for choosing chunk size and overlap. Overlap is essential if the thing we're looking for is correct at the cutoff when the chunks for the embeddings are created.

```
text_splitter =
RecursiveCharacterTextSplitter(chunk_size=1000,
chunk_overlap=100)
```

Chainlit uses decorators for code execution. We'll employ two of
them. The first is "@cl.on_chat_start," which is pretty self-
explanatory. Here, we set up some variables to receive the uploaded
PDF, set some parameters for file size and timeout, ask the user to
upload the file, and wait to receive it.

```
# Function triggered at the start of chat
@cl.on_chat_start
async def on_chat_start():
    # Request the user to upload a PDF file
    files = None
    while not files:
        files = await cl.AskFileMessage(
            content="Please upload a PDF file",
            accept=["application/pdf"],
            max_size_mb=25,
            timeout=180,
        ).send()

    file = files[0]
```

We'll notify the user that we're processing their uploaded file and save
it to the tmp directory.

```python
# Notifying the user about processing
processing_msg = cl.Message(
    content=f"Processing `{file.name}`...",
    disable_human_feedback=True
)
await processing_msg.send()

# Saving the uploaded file locally
if not os.path.exists("tmp"):
    os.makedirs("tmp")
with open(f"tmp/{file.name}", "wb") as f:
    f.write(file.content)
```

Next, we'll load the PDF, split it into chunks, and create the embeddings using OpenAI's embeddings API. We will notify the user once this process is complete.

```python
# Loading and splitting the PDF document
pdf_loader = PyPDFLoader(file_path=f"tmp/{file.name}")
documents =
pdf_loader.load_and_split(text_splitter=text_splitter)

# Creating embeddings for the documents
embeddings = OpenAIEmbeddings()
doc_search = await
cl.make_async(Chroma.from_documents)(documents,
embeddings)

# Inform the user about readiness
processing_msg.content = f"I am ready to answer
questions about `{file.name}`."
```

```
await processing_msg.update()
```

Next, we have a basic prompt template and a simple function to format
the uploaded file to prepare it for the model:

```
# Setting up the chat prompt template
prompt_template = ChatPromptTemplate.from_template(
    """Answer questions based on the following:
{context}

    Question: {question}"""
)

# Function to format document content
def format_docs(docs):
    return "\n\n".join([doc.page_content for doc in
docs])
```

We close out the "@cl.on_chat_start" section by defining our retriever,
chaining the whole process into a runnable, and setting a session
variable to keep track of the process as we chat with our PDF.

```
# Setting up the retriever and runnable
retriever = doc_search.as_retriever()
runnable = (
        {"context": retriever | format_docs, "question":
RunnablePassthrough()}
        | prompt_template
        | model
        | StrOutputParser()
```

```
)

# Storing the runnable in the user session
cl.user_session.set("runnable", runnable)
```

The other decorator we'll use is "@cl_on_message," which handles the messages as they return from the model. Here, we stream the response from the model and update the UI with the received responses.

```
# Function triggered upon receiving a message
@cl.on_message
async def on_message(message: cl.Message):
    # Retrieve the runnable from the user session
    runnable = cl.user_session.get("runnable")  # type:
Runnable

    # Create a message object for response
    response_msg = cl.Message(content="")
    await response_msg.send()

    # Stream the response from the runnable
    async for chunk in runnable.astream(
            message.content,

config=RunnableConfig(callbacks=[cl.LangchainCallbackHan
dler()]),
    ):
        await response_msg.stream_token(chunk)

    # Update the message with the final response
    await response_msg.update()
```

And there you have it! A fully functioning chatbot using retrieval augmented generation (RAG)!

We'll need to install the following:

```
pip install chainlit
pip install pypdf
pip install chromadb
pip install tiktoken
```

Launch your bot using the following command:

```
chainlit run app.py
```

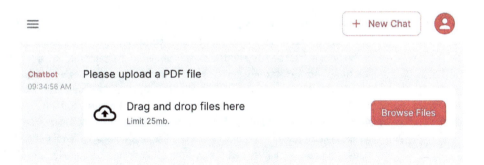

Chatbot
09:27:32 AM

Please upload a PDF file

09:28:04 AM

I am ready to answer questions about
`univerasal_declaration_of_human_rights.pdf` .

User
09:28:31 AM

What is this document about?

Chatbot
09:28:31 AM

This document is the Universal Declaration of Human Rights, which outlines the inherent dignity and equal and inalienable rights of all members of the human family. It emphasizes the importance of protecting human rights, promoting friendly relations between nations, and achieving universal respect for and observance of human rights and fundamental freedoms.

Took 2 steps ⌄

User
09:29:16 AM

What does is have to say about education?

Chatbot
09:29:16 AM

According to the given information, education is considered a fundamental right that everyone has. It should be directed towards the full development of the human personality and the strengthening of respect for human rights and freedoms. Education should promote understanding, tolerance, and friendship among all nations, racial or religious groups. Parents also have the right to choose the kind of education that shall be given to their children. Education should be free and at least elementary education should be compulsory. Technical and professional education should be made generally available, and higher education should be equally accessible to all on the basis of merit.

Took 2 steps ⌃

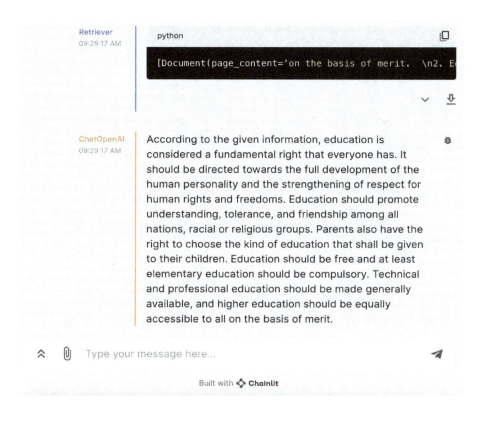

One of the great things you can do when using Chainlit is to click to expand on the steps taken to arrive at the response.

Completed RAG agent code:

```python
import os
import chainlit as cl
from langchain.embeddings import OpenAIEmbeddings
from langchain.chat_models import ChatOpenAI
from langchain.prompts import ChatPromptTemplate
from langchain.schema import StrOutputParser
```

```python
from langchain.document_loaders import PyPDFLoader
from langchain.text_splitter import
RecursiveCharacterTextSplitter
from langchain.vectorstores.chroma import Chroma
from langchain.schema.runnable import Runnable,
RunnablePassthrough, RunnableConfig

os.environ ["OPENAI_API_KEY"] = "<YOUR API KEY>"

model = ChatOpenAI(streaming=True)

text_splitter =
RecursiveCharacterTextSplitter(chunk_size=1000,
chunk_overlap=100)


# Function triggered at the start of chat
@cl.on_chat_start
async def on_chat_start():
    # Request the user to upload a PDF file
    files = None
    while not files:
        files = await cl.AskFileMessage(
            content="Please upload a PDF file",
            accept=["application/pdf"],
            max_size_mb=25,
            timeout=180,
        ).send()

    file = files[0]

    # Notifying the user about processing
```

```python
    processing_msg = cl.Message(
        content=f"Processing `{file.name}`...",
        disable_human_feedback=True
    )
    await processing_msg.send()

    # Saving the uploaded file locally
    if not os.path.exists("tmp"):
        os.makedirs("tmp")
    with open(f"tmp/{file.name}", "wb") as f:
        f.write(file.content)

    # Loading and splitting the PDF document
    pdf_loader =
PyPDFLoader(file_path=f"tmp/{file.name}")
    documents =
pdf_loader.load_and_split(text_splitter=text_splitter)

    # Creating embeddings for the documents
    embeddings = OpenAIEmbeddings()
    doc_search = await
cl.make_async(Chroma.from_documents)(documents,
embeddings)

    # Inform the user about readiness
    processing_msg.content = f"I am ready to answer
questions about `{file.name}`."
    await processing_msg.update()

    # Setting up the chat prompt template
    prompt_template = ChatPromptTemplate.from_template(
```

```python
    """Answer questions based on the following:
{context}

    Question: {question}"""
    )

    # Function to format document content
    def format_docs(docs):
        return "\n\n".join([doc.page_content for doc in
docs])

    # Setting up the retriever and runnable
    retriever = doc_search.as_retriever()
    runnable = (
            {"context": retriever | format_docs,
"question": RunnablePassthrough()}
            | prompt_template
            | model
            | StrOutputParser()
    )

    # Storing the runnable in the user session
    cl.user_session.set("runnable", runnable)


# Function triggered upon receiving a message
@cl.on_message
async def on_message(message: cl.Message):
    # Retrieve the runnable from the user session
    runnable = cl.user_session.get("runnable")  # type:
Runnable
```

```python
# Create a message object for response
response_msg = cl.Message(content="")
await response_msg.send()

# Stream the response from the runnable
async for chunk in runnable.astream(
        message.content,

config=RunnableConfig(callbacks=[cl.LangchainCallbackHan
dler()]),
    ):
        await response_msg.stream_token(chunk)

# Update the message with the final response
await response_msg.update()
```

Code for the projects in this book can be found here:

https://github.com/glenpatzlaff/langchain_book

About the author:

Glen Patzlaff is a Software Engineer and Technology Consultant who empowers individuals and professionals to harness the full potential of their technology. With 25+ years of experience in the tech industry, he is passionate about demystifying technology and AI, making it accessible and practical for everyone.

If you would like to connect, please reach out to me on LinkedIn: https://www.linkedin.com/in/gpatzlaff